Nā Pali

IMAGES OF KAUA'I'S NORTHWEST SHORE

Photography and text by

David Boynton

Mutual Publishing

ISBN-10: 1-56647-782-4
ISBN-13: 978-1-56647-782-6
Library of Congress Catalog Card Number:2006927635

Photographic assistance provided by Sue Boynton, who may be contacted at the web site: www.davidboyntonphotography.com

First Printing, October 2006
1 2 3 4 5 6 7 8 9

Mutual Publishing, LLC
1215 Center Street, Suite 210
Honolulu, Hawai'i 96816
Ph: 808-732-1709 / Fax: 808-734-4094
Email: info@mutualpublishing.com
www.mutualpublishing.com

Printed in China

Remote beaches, steep-walled valleys, and cathedral-like cliffs stretch thirteen miles along Kauaʻi's Nā Pali coast.

Golden sunsets highlight many an evening along Nā Pali,
which extends along the northwestern side of Kaua'i.

Huge winter surf crashes into steep cliffs,
undercutting the basalt lava until it collapses into the ocean.

Tropical greenery clothes the windward portion of Nā Pali,
which becomes more arid along its west-facing expanse.

Five million years of rainfall have carved jagged pinnacles
into the steep cliffs of Honopū Valley.

At the base of cliffs that loom high above Kēʻē Beach lies
an ancient heiau dedicated to Laka, goddess of hula.

Kaua'i's windward coastline is fringed with a wide expanse of reefs,
which are not present on the northern Nā Pali coast.

The calm lagoon at Kēʻē is a popular snorkeling site,
but swimmers need to be aware of dangerous, unseen currents.

Nā Pali begins where the road ends at Kēʻē Beach in Haʻēna on Kauaʻi's north shore.

One of the state's most popular and scenic hiking trails begins at Kē'ē Beach, and winds along steep slopes for two miles to Hanakāpī'ai Valley.

The Kalalau trail winds in and out of gulches past the distinctive
silhouettes of native hala (pandanus) trees.

Hanakāpīʻai Beach is the destination for most hikers on the Kalalau Trail;
a swim looks inviting, but strong currents have caused numerous drownings here.

Hardy hikers enjoy the challenge of a slippery two-mile trek
from Hanakāpīʻai Beach to a dramatic waterfall deep in the valley.

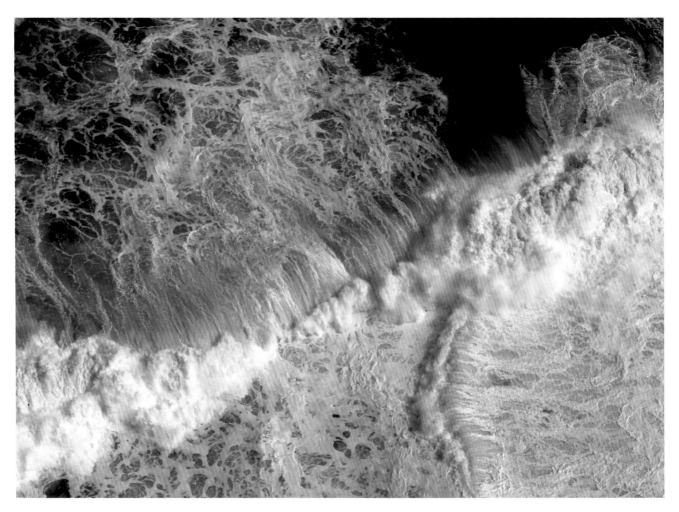

The trail along Nā Pali offers a wonderful and safe viewpoint
to observe the powerful crashing of winter waves.

Hanakāpī'ai's sandy beach disappears with the large surf of winter,
replaced by underlying basalt boulders.

Nā Pali cliffs have been undercut by millions of years of pounding waves,
which carve out sea caves in the volcanic strata.

White-tailed tropic birds (koaʻe kea) nest in the safety
of Nā Pali's steepness, in small cliff-face hollows.

Backpackers enjoy the challenge of a strenuous eleven-mile hike into Kalalau Valley.

Colorful morning glory (koali) flowers sprout from vines that festoon trailside shrubs and trees.

Kamehameha butterflies, one of only two native Hawaiian butterfly species,
are occasionally encountered along Kalalau trail.

Feral goats, which have greatly harmed native ecosystems,
easily negotiate steep Nā Pali cliffs.

The trail crosses folds of narrow ridges before heading down
an eroded landscape ("red hill") on the approach to Kalalau Valley.

Kalalau's sandy beach is a welcome sight as the last mile of trail rounds the final cliff.

A fortress of basalt pinnacles forms a backdrop to the Kalalau campground.

Many visitors choose to kayak rather than hike into Kalalau;
a permit is required for landing and camping.

Stone walls tell of ancient times when many hundreds of Hawaiians lived
in the richness of Kalalau's natural resources and beauty.

Kalalau Valley, as seen from a 4,000-feet elevation in Kōke'e State park,
is one of Hawai'i's most memorable vistas.

The twin beaches of Honopū Valley, just beyond Kalalau,
are connected by an eroded volcanic arch.

A small but cool and refreshing stream brings fresh water
under the arch and down to the beach of Honopū.

Sheer cliffs behind the dunes at Honopū Beach are home
to rare native plants; camping or landing here by boat is prohibited.

Knife-edged ridges descend from Honopū's precipitous
heights, taking on a warm blush in the late afternoon sun.

Scrubby shrubs, yellowing grasses, and red dirt characterize Nā Pali's arid leeward cliffs, in contrast to the lush greenery of the moist windward coast.

The viewpoint over Awa'awapuhi Valley, as seen from the end of a 3.5-mile trail in Kōke'e State Park, is one of Kaua'i's classic hiking destinations.

Beyond Awaʻawapuhi are the two valleys of Nuʻalolo;
the fringing reef of Nuʻalolo Kai is a remote but popular site for snorkeling.

Steep cliffs encompass the terraced walls of ancient taro fields in Nuʻalolo ʻĀina valley.

Taro plants still thrive in the small stream that winds
its way among ancient ruins in Nuʻalolo ʻĀina.

Stream water glistens as it tumbles over lava boulders in Nuʻalolo Stream.

Miloliʻi Valley descends precipitously between
ridges west of Kōkeʻe State Park.

The long sandy beach of Miloli'i provides a respite for green sea turtles
when big surf pounds the Nā Pali coastline.

Polihale, the state's longest beach, marks the western end of Nā Pali coast.

Great sunsets and room to roam make Polihale a favorite destination
for visitors and residents, but currents make swimming dangerous here.

Wave-cut cliffs seen from Polihale Beach continue all the way to Waimea, providing evidence of ancient sea level changes.

A full moon sets into pastel mists of the western
sky beyond Nā Pali at sunrise.